Reflections in My Spirit

Reflections in My Spirit

A Thirty-Day Devotional to Inspire Joy

REGINA McINTOSH

RESOURCE *Publications* • Eugene, Oregon

REFLECTIONS IN MY SPIRIT
A Thirty-Day Devotional to Inspire Joy

Copyright © 2024 Regina McIntosh. All rights reserved. Except for brief quotations in critical publications or reviews, no part of this book may be reproduced in any manner without prior written permission from the publisher. Write: Permissions, Wipf and Stock Publishers, 199 W. 8th Ave., Suite 3, Eugene, OR 97401.

Resource Publications
An Imprint of Wipf and Stock Publishers
199 W. 8th Ave., Suite 3
Eugene, OR 97401

www.wipfandstock.com

PAPERBACK ISBN: 978-1-6667-4114-8
HARDCOVER ISBN: 978-1-6667-4115-5
EBOOK ISBN: 978-1-6667-4116-2

03/29/24

Contents

Day 1 | 1
Day 2 | 3
Day 3 | 5
Day 4 | 7
Day 5 | 9
Day 6 | 11
Day 7 | 13
Day 8 | 15
Day 9 | 17
Day 10 | 19
Day 11 | 21
Day 12 | 23
Day 13 | 25
Day 14 | 27
Day 15 | 29
Day 16 | 31

Day 17 | 33
Day 18 | 35
Day 19 | 38
Day 20 | 40
Day 21 | 42
Day 22 | 44
Day 23 | 46
Day 24 | 48
Day 25 | 50
Day 26 | 52
Day 27 | 54
Day 28 | 56
Day 29 | 58
Day 30 | 60
I'm Always Smiling... | 62

Day 1

SINCE I CAN REMEMBER I've longed to see my words in print. It isn't as if I feel like I'm any more worthy or saved because I write poetry and prose intended to uplift Jesus. It isn't as if I feel like I can write my way into heaven because I know I can't. And, it isn't as if I think I am any closer to Jesus than the person reading these words because that all depends on your personal relationship with the Lord—not the ability to pour out your soul on a blank page. It's simply that I love to write and that comes with the hope that, sometime, someway, someone will read what I've written. I have had that hope for a long, long time, so when I first found someone willing to publish my inklings in their journals, I was excited, exhilarated and enlightened. I felt like the Lord had blessed me and, undoubtedly, He had.

There is always a blessing being poured out on the heart who loves Jesus and longs to do God's will. Blessings can range from having enough to being enough to giving enough. Blessings can come in hopes, dreams, ideas and even in the lingering inspiration or goodwill. Blessings can come in the sparkle of starlight and in the brilliance of sunlight. Blessings can come.. anywhere, anytime, through anyone. They come, most often though, to the heart who loves and that is something I have found that I must do to feel close to the One who saved my soul—Love! Just love.

I hope you discover love drenching these empty pages, filling them with a light that is so bright you couldn't dim it even if you tried. I pray that you find grace in these reflections, these pearls—and a song that you can sing on your way to reach out toward your own dreams.

Day 1

Writing has blessed me and my hope is, that with each of these short writings, you are blessed too! With that, I will move on to page two!

Matthew 13:45–46 (KJV) 45 Again, the kingdom of heaven is like unto a merchant man, seeking goodly pearls: 46 Who, when he had found one pearl of great price, went and sold all that he had, and bought it.

PRAYER

Live through me, precious Savior. Show me what to say, what to do and when the time comes, who to give the music you sing to me, the pearls you have poured through my heart and soul, leaving me with the hope that these words find a ear who will know these pearls are the ones that can make life better, silence the bitter and promise the beauty. These pages, these pearls, are the ones that you've given me—please bless them if and when they touch the hearts of those willing to listen as they read through my witnessing.

Day 2

WINTER IS A TIME for rest. The flowers rest from their flamboyant displays. Trees take off their garments and await the warmth of spring to show off their wardrobe again. The animals hibernate and people stay by the fire instead of the air conditioner. It is a time of rest, a time of waiting, a time of prayer and praise, rejuvenating.

Prayers of praise flow through the empty days as the moon and stars shimmer in the evening and sunlight falls across the snow covered lawns during the daylight hours. Prayers linger on hearts who long to grow closer, discover a more intimate relationship with the God of the universe, and listen to the whispers of hope that beckon souls through the silence that brings grace to our lives.

When I pray, during the Winter, I pray for a faith that is resilient and wise, a faith that lights up hearts and lives, a faith that delights and abides, a faith that shines through the twinkle in my eyes. I long to share my faith with others who also need to feel the rich blessing of a spiritual connection to the One who gave us life and continues to give us life long after His amazing sacrifice.

As I pray, this Winter, I pray for the chance to give back to the God who made me, the One who saved me and the One who awaits me in heaven where I will one day accompany Him and praise Him eternally. My winter prayers are more like candles breathing light across my memories, uplifting and promising that He will listen as sincerely and serenely as the faith that calls me to pray without ceasing and praise without a reason. . . to praise simply because He is Jesus!

Day 2

Psalms 147:1 Praise ye the LORD: for it is good to sing praises unto our God; for it is pleasant; and praise is comely.

PRAYER

Thank You, God—for the light, the love, the longing in my soul for a relationship with the One You sent to this world, the only One who can bring me through the darkness, into the light of Your glory. The wonder of Your Son is the reason that I have for giving back these heartfelt writings—these pearls from my heart, the same heart You blessed with more kindness than I could ever possibly thank You for. Thank You, God—for these pearls of love. I only pray that they're a help to someone.

Day 3

REST—TAKING A BREATH—IS HARD to do sometimes. It seems like I should be doing—like Martha. I feel like I need to cook or wipe away handprints on some surface, dust something or apply a fresh coat of paint to a wall. It feels like I need to be doing something with my every movement, my every moment. But Jesus didn't agree.

When Martha told Jesus her sister, Mary, wasn't helping her with the work, Jesus rebuked her. He told her that she was anxious and fretted about the work, but that Mary had chosen the good thing by sitting at His feet and listening to Him. Mary listened. And, once again, like Martha, I find that I have trouble simply listening. But it is through listening that we learn, grow and become the people God meant for us to be when He created us in the womb.

Listening takes effort for some people—indeed, for me. I have to take a moment away from my errands or routines to hear what my husband or someone else is saying. Sometimes that might even mean reading between the lines and hearing what they don't actually say. It may mean taking the time to hear and understand what they mean when they say something, reading between the lines of their body language and facial gestures. Reading between the lines takes time and truly listening.

I know I've failed to listen. My husband often tells me "You don't listen" and I have to agree with him. I don't! But, I should and I can if I take a moment and give the listening my best effort. I have to take a breather, a moment away from my chore or task, a moment to hear what is being said, to pay attention, and give back to the speaker with my full interest. And, I've learned, through much

Day 3

trial and error, that if I listen with complete concentration, I learn and it is often through this learning that I discover some blessing that Jesus had meant me to have for a long while—if I had only taken a breath and simply listened!

Luke 10:42 (KJV) But one thing is needful: and Mary hath chosen that good part, which shall not be taken away from her.

PRAYER

Lord, please know my heart and the workings of my soul, whisper Your light through my thoughts and remind me that, with You, my joy will be fulfilled. When I listen to Your still, small voice and know the blessing, the beauty, the best that will never be taken away when I humbly sit at your feet, like Mary did, and listen to those things You will give me with Your amazing kindness, your insight, your spirit—I can know, if I listen, You will give me everything I need to feel You, Your presence, Your Holy Spirit—standing with me, within me.

Day 4

I WAS EATING DINNER with a friend last night and we were talking about the times we'd thought 'now surely God can't forgive me for what I've done this time' but she reminded me of something her preacher had said. He said, "He's a God of second chances" and oh my goodness, this is absolute truth, a fact that I (and many others) are so very thankful for. He certainly IS a God of second chances.

He gave me a second chance the time I spoke ill of someone, the time I was a horrid gossip, the time I let the light fall away from my soul. He gave me a second chance when I wasn't pleasant or kind, when I didn't allow Him to control my mind, when I was filled with anger, resentment or bitter dislike. He gave me a second chance when I failed to listen to Him in prayer, when I let someone down and when I let Him down, when I was less than honest and felt the lie fall from my lips and my heart. He gave me a second chance when I didn't deserve the grace in His gift, the blessing that He gives me with each breath I take.

If I hadn't had those second chances you know where I'd be today. Probably lying in a gutter somewhere with a bottle pressed to my lips, trying to gentle the sorrows and grief, let go of the anger or find some kind of relief. If He wasn't a God of second chances, I'd never have known the joy of His presence, the kindness I so treasure, the warmth of His love falling over my spirit and soothing away all the darkness.

I'm so very thankful for a God who gives me second chances. I don't always get it right the first time and, in all truth, I seldom get it right the first time. I do have the ability to learn, though, to learn and grow. And, that is just what I've done, thanks to a God

Day 4

who forgives and gives me another chance to begin again. This God of second chances is the God who I love more and more. The farther I go in this life, the more my love for Him grows.

John 8:10 When Jesus had lifted up himself, and saw none but the woman, he said unto her, Woman, where are those thine accusers? hath no man condemned thee?

PRAYER

You, precious Jesus, have loved me like that woman who was caught in adultery. Even though I was caught, red handed, in my sin—You offered me grace that, in spite of my yearning for this very grace, I can't possibly comprehend. It is Your grace and mercy, Your love, that reminds me, when I mess up—and I don't think there is any way You can forgive what I've done—YOU forgive me. You love me with a love that is more beautiful than anything in this world. Indeed, Your love is not of this world. It is a love that is divine and abides with those who know You as Savior. Thank You, dear Jesus, for forgiving me of everything I thought was unforgivable.

Day 5

THERE ARE TIMES WHEN I fail to appreciate the things in my life that are so typical, so simple and so usual that I, quite simply, fail to notice or be thankful for them. These come in something so amazing as a tangerine sun or a twinkling star to a soft rainfall or a melodious robin. The simple blessings are often the ones I find myself taking for granted. And, I can't help thinking it is that way for many others. Simplicity is taken for granted despite our best efforts to remember these amazing joys and thank God for His generosity.

The sound of a familiar voice, the laughter of a friend, the smile on someone's heart, the penetrating faith that leaves me feeling so fortunate. There are hopes and dreams that relieve and restore invaluable kindness' that cause me so much happiness, joys that inspire, faith that doesn't require any explanation, only acceptance and the grace that comes from its touch. There are wisdoms, biblical truths and visions, intimacies and inspirations, enlightenment and imagination. There is a light that fills the soul with love that can't be voiced, love so alive it isn't a choice. It is simply life falling soft across the night.

As the skies darken at sunset, breathing a melody of richest yearnings through the soul who is churning, hoping beyond hope that there is a blessing falling down from heaven, pouring out grace across a life. As I listen to the wind blow and feel the kiss of its whisper touch my cheek, I know that I have something greater than money or material possessions. I have hope and faith and love that knows only giving like a sweet, gentle affection that desires

Day 5

to cover hearts with acceptance, a blessing like no one could even imagine.

Many times I fail to appreciate the blessings that flow gently through my life—little things like rain and sunshine, grace and faith, love that breaks through the darkness sending my entire life a light that shimmers like the holiest love God might give. I fail Him, you see, by not seeing the blessings in my life. Yet, I please Him with my belief!

Luke 17:17 And Jesus answering said, Were there not ten cleansed? but where are the nine?

PRAYER

Dear God, the One who holds the sun and moon, the One who knows each star by name, the One who remembers me from the womb. . . Dear God, please forgive me when I forget gratitude. When I go about my business without thanking You for everything You do, for all the gifts, the little things, the simple joys and amazing grace—when I forget to say Thank YOU, dear God—please forgive me and remind me, You are the One who my heart owes its beating, my breath its breathing, my soul its singing. You, heavenly Father, are the One who I owe all my thanks to. And, I do,—I thank You for it all, but most of all, dear God, I thank You for YOU!

Day 6

THERE WAS A TIME when I didn't listen to the still, small voice that is the Holy Spirit revealing His instructions to me. I wasn't always filled with the desire to listen and be who I hope God intends for me to be. I wasn't always happier about going to church than going to the ballgame. I wasn't always seeking the Creator's good will for me. I wasn't always the woman I am today and if I could go back to yesterday, when I didn't listen to God's voice instructing me, I would go there and listen with all my heart and soul. I would do those things that I know God had for me to do. I would fulfill the destiny He had for me if I had only been the child who sought to follow Him with all my heart.

I didn't always listen, but now, I do. I listen when He whispers for me to write a poem or read a book. I listen when He tells me I should watch a certain movie or, too, when I shouldn't watch a certain movie. I listen when He gives me instructions on just what to say in a conversation with my boss. I listen when He reminds me of the times when I refused to listen and those times when I most definitely wish I had listened. I listen to that still, small voice and when I don't hear His voice, I pray.

I pray for conviction, for enlightenment, for understanding, for wisdom. I pray that He is listening to me and will eventually lead me in the way that He intends for me. I pray for my light to give off a reflection of His spirit. I pray for grace, for hope, for peace, for more faith that I can imagine. I pray for Him to pour out His spirit on everything that I come into contact with and give me the assurance that He has taken it upon Himself to prepare the way

Day 6

for me. I pray and He listens and when He isn't listening, I know He is speaking.

Therefore, it is then, that I LISTEN!

1 Kings 19:12 (KJV) And after the earthquake a fire; but the Lord was not in the fire: and after the fire a still small voice.

PRAYER

Lord, I know I don't always listen. I know I'm not always good. I know that I don't always do the right thing, show the love You have anointed me to show, shine the light that You put in my soul. I know, precious Lord, that I'm not always the best child. I know all of these things, yet I still turn to You with every need. I turn to You when I bleed. I turn to You because it is YOU who I believe. You promised me love that would never forsake me and, even though I'm so flawed and imperfect, I listened. I heard You when You told me You would love me through my darkest moments, through my messes and my mistakes, with a love that is eternal, a love that I will always thank You for. Thank You, Lord, for that still, small voice that still gets through to me when my life is chaotic and all I can pray is "Please help me, Lord." Thank You, Lord—You are my everything and more—You're the blessing of real love!

Day 7

WHEN I WAS GROWING up I went to a Freewill Baptist Church where they sang old timey hymns, had Sunday school classes and listened to the preacher preach with a passion reserved for Sunday morning and life altering messages. It was a good church and I went to the alter when I was a young girl, gave my heart to Jesus and laid my burdens down.

Still, I sinned. And I probably sinned more often after I'd been saved than I did prior to being saved. I couldn't seem to find the strength to overcome the way many Christians can. I was stuck in the muddy puddle of sinning that seemed to be the only way I could go. I was a sinner saved by grace yet I was as weak as anyone could possibly be. I was weak all the way down to my pleas for a second chance, for spiritual atonement, for grace through faith in my Savior, the Lord Jesus Christ.

Life moved quickly and I was in and out of church over the next years. I found myself crawling out of sin more often than I did sitting on the church pews of my youth. I cried and I begged and I cried some more. Still, I was lost and I couldn't find the peace that I knew came to others who had been saved.

Finally, I poured out my heart and soul to this Jesus who I knew held my hope in His hand. I asked Him to help me to heal from the wounds of my past and to find a road that would lead me toward redemption instead of the failure I'd known. And, to my great surprise and delight, He did just that. As I slowly learned to follow Him, He led me down a path rich with hope, faith and love—a path that I could have traveled long before if I'd only listened to the wisdom in the Scriptures.

Day 7

It takes longer for some of us. But, when I found Him, I found love!

Luke 15:4 (KJV) What man of you, having an hundred sheep, if he lose one of them, doth not leave the ninety and nine in the wilderness, and go after that which is lost, until he find it?

PRAYER

Heavenly Father, Thank YOU for coming for me, the lost sheep, so many times. Thank You for never letting me go, despite the dark mire that clung to me and left me stuck so often. Thank You for embracing me when all was said and done, for never forsaking me—even though that is just what I deserved. Thank You for inviting me to enjoy the fatted calf with You, even after I'd gone my own way and struggled through things that prevented me from listening to the promises You gave me when You blessed me with a love that is filled with grace and mercy, a love that I can only believe because You gave me Your only Son—the whole reason that forgiveness came to me, the sinner who fell before You, the same one you pulled from the muck and cleaned up in ways that I couldn't have imagined for me. Thank You, Father—for grace, for faith, for the love that saved my soul—for the One who saves everyone He knows!

Day 8

I'VE HEARD THE IDIOM, to take life with an "attitude of gratitude." I think this is one of the better sayings I've happened upon during my lifetime. I like this way of saying that we need to be thankful for all that we've been blessed with. I couldn't agree more. I am, definitely, one more thankful lady. I feel so grateful for everything that has happened in my life—even those things that I didn't believe I could ever be thankful for, like a divorce, a job loss, a failure or doubt.

If I hadn't ever had that divorce, I wouldn't have ever had the chance to become the wife of a man I feel so close to, so amazed by, and so blessed to know. He is the husband of my dreams. He brings hope and joy and peace into my life and blesses my soul in more ways than I can write down in one sitting. He is a ray of light that pierces through the darkness and colors my whole world in beauty. He is a reflection of grace and a wonder who amazes me in every way. And, if I hadn't ever struggled through my divorce, I wouldn't have become his wife.

So, yes, I'm even thankful for those times when I didn't think I could get by. Those times when I was lost in grief and pain, when I didn't think I'd ever smile again, when laughter was a stranger and I didn't believe God could possibly bless me with this horrendous battle.

God blesses to the uttermost, though. He blesses when you least expect the blessing, with a love that is alive with kindness and affection. He is an awesome God who calls out to the heart and soul with a light that always reflects joy and compassion, a warmth that will comfort, heal and protect you. His blessings go above and

Day 8

beyond perfection. They are the connection to the heart of One who knows just what we're going through and pours out a blessing that will penetrate even the toughest walls. He is the blessing who is alive!

1 Corinthians 13:12 (KJV) For now we see through a glass, darkly; but then face to face: now I know in part; but then shall I know even as also I am known.

PRAYER

Dear Lord, Forgive me for those times when I've struggled to understand Your will for me, when I didn't think You could possibly know what You were doing because the pain was too great or the shame too dreadful. Forgive me, dear Lord, for refusing to see that YOUR ways are higher than my ways and YOU know what I need much better than I do. You give me—not what I deserve—but what You preserve, especially for me. You know my heart and soul intimately and You offer me the best when I can't possibly pass the test. Thank You, Lord, for giving me, not what I want—but what I need and what will bring me, ultimately, to a better future than I might have thought possible. Thank You, dear Lord, for the love you bring me even when I'm feeling so unworthy and uncertain. Thank YOU, Lord—for grace that sees through my hopes into the heart of my dreams where I know a love that shines brighter than the most beautiful joy. Thank You, Lord—for loving me!

Day 9

BEFORE I REALIZED JUST how much God loves me—before I felt the amazing grace that has been poured out on me. . . before I knew Him the way I do today, I was always searching.

I combed the hearts and souls of most everyone I came into contact with, explored the highs and lows of addictions and depression and mania, felt my thoughts fading into the shadows of a darkness so compelling it could actually be touched.

I sought every part of my life, be it good or bad or insightful, for the love that I was emersed in when I discovered for myself that Jesus truly is my everything and He truly does satisfy every want or need. This Jesus I had failed so often gave me love that couldn't be described or explained, love so gentle it left me filled with tenderness and faith, love so strong that I couldn't turn it off no matter how often I let sin slip into my heart. Love so alive it felt the need to testify!

When I look back today, I don't know why I sought this abiding love in so many other places besides the one place where I could find it. I suppose I was a little slow to learn the amazing truth about Jesus. He is the rock, the promise, the light that outshines all others. He is hope, faith and love all wrapped up in One, the only One who is worthy of my heart and soul, my complete surrender. His is a love that compels me to believe when I can't see a way and to know when I don't know. I know that He brings peace and as long as I depend on Him, I will have everything I could possibly need.

Day 9

Jesus brought me through the searching into victory and the knowledge that He is worthy of my soul! I BELIEVE—I KNOW He holds my heart and soul in His hands and He always understands!

1 Corinthians 15:57 (KJV) But thanks be to God, which giveth us the victory through our Lord Jesus Christ.

PRAYER

Dear Lord, when I was torn between doubt and sorrow, when the skies were endless clouds and I couldn't see the hope for tomorrow, when everywhere I looked—I saw pain and disillusionment, You were near. You breathed hope into my spirit, sent faith so that I wouldn't give up, gave me assurance that the doubts wouldn't win and I'd find a way to feel the SON once again. When I wasn't inspired or inspiring—when I was living in the shadow of failure—when everywhere I looked, I could see disaster, YOU gave me hope. You showed me that there was a way, despite all my doubts. You led me through the discouragement in my heart. You SAVED me and You continue to save me when I'm lost, when I hurt, when I don't know the path. You are the light that saved my soul and I'll always be thankful that You brought the victory with You when You shined love that is my greatest hope. Thank You, dear Lord, for the victory, for the peace, for the chance to experience a love like this.

Day 10

My uncle Michael, who was always like a big brother because he was so young when I was born—12 years old and excited about the baby his big sister had delivered. He gave me his kind heart and gentle words all through my life. He was a friend when I was sad and a godsend when I felt alone. He didn't ever make me feel like I was less than or not enough. He made me feel like everything I did or said was worth something. And, I loved him with all my heart.

The doctors told me, "He is in a lot of pain" and I am still not sure what sort of pain he might have felt because he had good parents, my beloved grandparents, who cherished him and gave him all their support. He had a good life. I don't know why he was in pain and I don't know why he was addicted to drugs and alcohol. He was though. He definitely was addicted and the disease was stronger than the hope that kept him looking for a way past the pain.

I tried with everything in me to save him and it was like I was losing my beloved brother the morning they told me he had passed into eternity. I was more than shaken. I was more than heartbroken. I was actually devastated. My heart felt so heavy I didn't think I could even cry out to God, but I did cry out. I cried out, "Why, Lord? WHY?" and even when I didn't get an answer, I knew that I had to find a way to deal with this grief or become as self-destructive as the man who had just passed into the next life.

It was months and even years before I could let go of the grief I felt when I lost Michael. He was gone and I was more alone in the world now without him. I felt like I'd been dealt a harsh blow but I prayed and I prayed some more and finally, I realized that God has

Day 10

this. God is in control of the entire universe and he is in control of death too. He knew my heartbreak and, even though I didn't know how to ask for His comfort, He still comforted me. His light is forever reflected in my hopes and dreams, and yes—in my doubts and beliefs—in my soul.

Isaiah 53:10 (KJV) Yet it pleased the Lord to bruise him; he hath put him to grief: when thou shalt make his soul an offering for sin, he shall see his seed, he shall prolong his days, and the pleasure of the Lord shall prosper in his hand.

PRAYER

Dear Lord, I don't always understand what You are doing. I can't see the moon and stars because the gloom clouds my view. I don't know what to do or where to turn when I feel so lost and alone—yet, I always find myself in Your presence, praying for Your kindness, Your blessings. Deep down, despite my grief and pain, I know that I can come to You with anything I feel, anything I need, anything that troubles me—and You will always answer my prayers. Even when the answers don't always come at once and when the answers aren't just what I hoped they would be, they still bring me through the storms and, most importantly, into a closer relationship with You, the One who holds the truth. Thank You, Lord, for bringing me hope when I didn't know what to do. Thank You, Lord, for silencing my worries and singing joy through my soul when I thought I wouldn't ever hear the music again. Thank You, Lord, for comforting me with Your wonderful peace. Thank You, Lord—for loving me!

Day 11

I haven't always listened. There have been times when I ignored the best advice and chose to take my own road. A road, I might add, that led to pain, sorrow and regret. Even though others were standing back, shaking their heads at my folly, I continued down a path that led me straight to mountains of despair and darkness.

One of these times happened when I was quite young. I had become friends with a girl who smoked. And, as you probably already guessed, I decided to take up smoking. It seemed harmless enough. All I was doing was inhaling a little nicotine into my system. What could it really hurt? Afterall, nearly all my family smoked. And even though they were a little older than me, my age shouldn't make that much difference.

My mom didn't smoke. She had tried smoking, she told me, when she was young, and didn't like it one little bit. She found the ashtrays sitting around the house from Dad's cigarettes beyond disgusting but she did put up with it. Just like I was sure she'd eventually see her way clear to accepting the fact that I had grown fond of Marlboro reds.

Little did I know and I'm not sure it would have stopped me if I had known, it would be approximately 35 years before I took my last puff from a Marlboro and finally (with a LOT of help from Jesus) kicked the habit that had plagued me for some of my teen years and all of my adult life. I quit in 2013 and today, I can't imagine what it was that made me so dependent on cigarettes.

Needless to say, the girl I became friends with. . ... Well, I'm pretty sure that she still smokes and, although I pray for her best, I

Day 11

know she will possibly die without kicking the habit because, like me, she doesn't always listen.

Proverbs 1:5 (KJV) A wise man will hear, and will increase learning; and a man of understanding shall attain unto wise counsels:

PRAYER

Dear Lord, I know I don't always listen to Your still, small voice. I don't always hear when You mention something relevant. I don't always heed Your advice or remember the miracle of Your sacrifice. Still—I listen to Your spirit when it reveals to me—something far more beautiful than I could have expected, something far more wise than I could have predicted, something far more kind than anything I might have imagined or thought of. Even when I don't listen, I still know Your light will guide me through the darkness and manifest itself in every doubt I might face, inspiring me to believe despite my lack of hearing. When I fail to listen, Lord, please don't fail to give me Your grace. Because it is Your grace, Your Spirit, that reminds my heart of its blessings. And, it is Your grace and Your Spirit that still reassures me, even when I can't hear You.

Day 12

WHEN I FOUND OUT I was bipolar, I was relieved. Relieved to finally have a diagnosis for the craziness in my life. Since I could remember, I'd felt 'crazy'. My mom, forever my ally, often told me that I was not crazy and that I shouldn't call myself crazy. She didn't like it when my ex-husband, who had been privy to much of my craziness, called me crazy. But, in all truth, I felt crazy. And, when I was finally diagnosed with bipolar disorder, I had my proof that there truly was a method to my insanity.

When I went into the hospital I was so out of it (not from drugs but from the mania) that I don't even remember some of the days I was there. They kept me there, in the hospital, under lock and key, until they'd had time to evaluate how the medicine they gave me would affect me. During that time, I called my mom every night. But, I called Jesus every few minutes. He was my anchor in the storm and I couldn't have possibly made it through that darkness of the soul without Him leading me. His light was a reflection I often looked to for support, wisdom and answers, His love was the wonder that saved me in more ways than one. He did, honestly, save me from myself.

God led me through the craziness and gave me reason to believe that I could achieve my dreams. And, amazingly, I have achieved more in the past few years—with the help of Jesus and medicine—than I achieved in the 40+ years before I knew I was bipolar. I am a work in progress but God has done wonders with the life that I have now. He has blessed me with a joy so beautiful that I often feel like thanking him profusely and I do. I thank Him in prayers, in thoughts and in deeds. I thank Him with the faith

Day 12

that allows me to give back to Him—my heart and soul, my hope and faith, the love that is a gift of His amazing grace. The love that is my greatest teacher, my greatest comfort, my greatest blessing. The love that is, actually, Jesus!

2 Corinthians 1:4 (KJV) Who comforteth us in all our tribulation, that we may be able to comfort them which are in any trouble, by the comfort wherewith we ourselves are comforted of God.

PRAYER

Dear Lord, thank You for loving me through my craziness, for making a way for me, for silencing the doubt in me and giving me grace to relieve my heart and soul. You have been the comfort when I couldn't find peace, the inspiration when I couldn't find my muse, the encouragement when I was so disheartened. You made sure that, even in the middle of the chaos, the mania—I knew what it meant to feel loved, to feel blessed. You didn't ever stop giving me a reason to believe and, through Your love, I knew—even in the darkness—a light that stirred to life all the joy that I know begins with the love that You pour out on those who know You. Thank YOU, dear Lord, for giving me the chance to know You, Holy Spirit, the wonder—the friend—the light that reflects all the beauty of the spirit You send to comfort me through the worst there is.

Day 13

I WAS NEARLY 50 when I started college and, even though I was older than most of my classmates, I discovered that life on a college campus can be very stimulating. All that learning seems to motivate, not only the mind, but also the heart. I felt a genuine love, joy and appreciation for those I came to know through my time at school.

Some of the folks I encountered while there were pursuing classes because they hoped to, not only better themselves in material ways, but for the simple purpose of following their dreams. Some of us, myself included, had dreamed of going to college and even if that time didn't lead to the best job or more material wealth, it would assuredly lead to the satisfaction of realizing a sought after dream.

It was hard work, though. I didn't ever realize that going to school could take up so much of my time. I spent morning, noon and night—every moment I wasn't sleeping or working at my part time job, reading academic books or writing scholarly papers for my classes. And, what time I wasn't doing those two things, I was praying for the ability to make it through another test or temptation. And, yes, even at my age, there are still temptations for His children.

Finally, in 2015, I graduated with honors (something that came after a long, hard road through the trials that come with heavy learning experiences). After those years of chasing that dream, I was a little lost when I was faced with just going to a job and not facing a new, difficult challenge on a daily basis. Suddenly, life seemed tedious. But that didn't last long.

Day 13

It was only a few weeks after graduation that I went to a new job, a new challenge and a new test of my faith. Thanks to Jesus and His outpouring of love, I have had more dreams come true that I can say!

Psalm 37:4 (KJV) Delight thyself also in the Lord: and he shall give thee the desires of thine heart.

PRAYER

Dear Lord, when I forget to say thank You for all You've given me, please forgive me and remind me—Your blessings truly are new every morning. You give me hope, peace, faith and grace. You give me joy, light, insight and love. You give me blessings that stir up the dreams in my heart and, then, give me the capacity to fulfill those dreams with strength that could only come from You, the One who makes a way where there seems to be no way. You are the One who awakens all my hopes and fulfills them, too, with Your amazing kindness, wisdom and authority. You are the ONE who I love with everything in me and I want to thank You, always, for making my every dream a reality.

Day 14

I don't like to watch tv that much. I know that it's a wonderful device but often when I sit down to watch a program I find myself thinking of all the things I could be doing other than watching tv. I could be, for instance, writing a poem or devotional. I could be using my energy for good things instead of searching through the channels hoping to find one that displays something besides drugs, drinking or other dark details that ring with words like depression, dread and despair.

Still, I do like Christian movies. When I find a movie that is about something I can relate to—like a follower finding peace, motivation, insight on inspiration, it peaks my interest. And, when I find a movie or program where someone is seeking, reaching out toward the light that is Jesus, my heart skips a beat as I turn up the volume on the remote. This is my kind of tv, my kind of joy, my kind of grace. I love Jesus and the love I feel for Him never fades.

Even though I'm not a avid tv watcher, there are programs on that device that call out to me the way the darkness calls for the light. And I tune in when the program is something that speaks to me. I also tune in to a heart who calls out to me. When someone I know (or for that matter don't know) mentions their love for the Father, the joy they've found in Jesus, or a scripture that resonates through my soul, my interest is picked and I listen to what they're saying.

This morning at work, I met a new follower of Christ and he was passionate about His faith. Inspired, I told him to never stop praying, reaching out to the One who saved him and made a way for him. As we parted, I felt the wonderful presence of the Holy

Day 14

Spirit surround me with a joy, a love, that can only be found in the One who came down from above to shine His light into the hearts of those who love because He first loved us. Much better than tv—this was a blessing so sweet it fed my spirit with His amazing grace.

John 14:16 (KJV) And I will pray the Father, and he shall give you another Comforter, that he may abide with you for ever;

PRAYER

Dear Lord, thank you for bringing other Christians into my life, Christians who show me that Your grace is always there, abiding in the hearts and souls of those who know You intimately, those who love You unconditionally and those who believe You with faith that is alive and fulfills every hope for love that is this beautiful, this inspiring, this gentle and real. Your love, sweet Savior. . . love falling over the spirit from the One You sent to us to comfort our hearts and spirits—this is a love that is beyond description. This is a love that silences every fear, holds onto the hope that He is near, fills the soul with a joy that is forever aware, with Him, there is joy beyond explanation, a joy that abides through every tear, always, throughout the years. With You, dear Lord, there is abundant love, love that is forever and always, love that testifies because Your love is worth everything—it is life!

Day 15

TEARS WEREN'T ALWAYS MY friends. There was a time when they poured out of me the way words do today. Even then, I wrote my heart out, but my heart wasn't nearly as sure of it's focus as it is today and when I pray, I always thank the Lord for His amazing grace, His life sustaining faith and His love that kept me sane when I felt more like I was insane than I can say.

Those teardrops weren't only the reflection of just how miserable I was then but also a reminder that I couldn't even control my own tears. I was at the mercy of those tears the way I'm at the mercy of my Creator today. Instead of feeling like I'm insane though, today I feel more sane than I've ever felt in my life and I'm certain that has more to do with my spiritual strength than anything else. Just as I believe my lack of spiritual strength birthed those many tears that poured out of me all those years ago.

Today, the more I pray, the closer I get to the One who holds the key to my life, the more sure I am that I have what it takes to make it through any battle that might come, any spiritual war, any discouragement, doubt or worry. I can make it through because I know the One, intimately, who makes a way where no way can be seen. The One who colors my heart in hues of joy and peace. The One who stirs up my dreams and feeds them with belief. The One who is the answer to my every need.

Without Him, I would be back to square one, pouring out a ocean of tears from a heart that is uncertain. But with Him, I am free to be the woman He intended me to be when He created me. I am free to be confidant, strong, hopeful. I am free to love without conditions and listen to the wonder of His Holy Spirit as it moves me to follow my dreams.

Revelation 21:4 (KJV) And God shall wipe away all tears from their eyes; and there shall be no more death, neither sorrow, nor crying, neither shall there be any more pain: for the former things are passed away.

PRAYER

Dear Lord, You know me better than I know myself and you know when the tears flow and when the tears are only lingering in my soul. You know my ups and downs, my smiles and frowns, the joy and pain. You see inside my heart in a way that I can't even see myself. You know what will bring me hope and faith and what will discourage my dreams. You are the One who silences my doubts and inspires my believing so that when I feel You near, I can also feel Your hand of grace wiping away those tears that were my anguish and sorrow, all the hurt that darkened my thoughts and feelings, the pain that was a reminder of my failure to let go of my selfish needs and pray for the peace in other's lives, those who were much worse off than me, the same ones who I forget when I only think of me. Thank you, Lord, for knowing me and loving me—even when I am only thinking of me!

Day 16

IT'S ALWAYS BEEN IN the quiet moments, when I'm alone but not lonely, when I am seeking with, not just my mind, but my heart, when I feel Him with me. His presence comes flowing over my spirit like a dream pursues me in sleep. It is a potent, dynamic weight pressing in on me gently, calmly, beautifully. It makes me feel like I am being hugged by Jesus and I suppose it is true—I am being hugged by the One who makes me whole!

His presence fills me up with energy and faith, hope and inspiration, a song of light and laughter, assurance that He is past, present and the hereafter. He is so wise that He never interferes when I am with someone else and need to listen to them or share my heart with them. He waits until I'm by myself to come to me quietly, gently, content to pursue my soul with a calm that is mellow and whispers through my thoughts. He isn't pushy, my Jesus. No. He isn't pushy. He is a true gentleman.

His way is mild and soothing. He brings peace with Him when He comes and fills the very air with a soft, easy restfulness that reminds me how amazing He can be. It is only through my faith that He allows me to see—He truly is the way, the truth, the life—the light of my life!

Once, when I was alone, I felt His Holy Spirit fall down on my heart and soul like rainfall, blessing me with a more intimate sense of Him than I'd ever experienced. It felt like every worry, every fear, every doubt and every year melted away from my mind and I was blessed with a peace that surely did pass all understanding, a peace that bathed me in joy beyond words, joy that I can only dream of most days. This joy was like being hugged by the One

Day 16

who makes all things new, gives hope to the hopeless and renews the spirit with serenity that is like a brilliant promise singing on the soul. This is the whisper of His spirit filling me!

Acts 20:24 (KJV) But none of these things move me, neither count I my life dear unto myself, so that I might finish my course with joy, and the ministry, which I have received of the Lord Jesus, to testify the gospel of the grace of God.

PRAYER

Dear Lord, to know You, to experience You, Your presence, Your light, Your peace and grace—the love that silences every doubt I meet—this is the meaning of love that is eternal, love that is alive and abundant, love that comes to those in need and supplies the joy that completes. In the center of my soul, I know the wonder of being in a relationship with the most amazing person there has ever been, the person of Jesus—my hope, my peace, my joy—my friend, the One who makes me see that love is alive and is filling me with a spirit that only You, my best friend, can bring to me. I'm so thankful to know the One who holds the heart and soul, who knows the way to glory, who is the light of the whole world. I'm so thankful to know that He is with me and He will always give me the wisdom to seek Him when I don't know the reason, the insight to believe when I can't see, the understanding to worship when I'm filled with grief. I'm so very thankful that I can always call on the One who stirs my soul to knowing that He is always with me, always protecting me and always accepting me. His love is my light and my life, the reason my soul can smile. And, I'm thankful, so thankful for Jesus.

Day 17

SOMETIMES I PUT THE cart before the horse. I get in a hurry and I forget what is important. I'll ask someone for a favor and totally ignore the need to uplift them. It only seems right that if you're going to expect something you should give something even if that something is only an encouragement or prayer, a reminder that you truly do care. And, I truly do care. It's just that, like I said, I sometimes fail to remember the importance of showing someone that I care.

I have to repent, usually at least once a day, for being so selfish. I might not mean to be selfish but that doesn't stop me one little bit from being selfish. I will reach out to someone with a need or plea for prayer or some kind of help and simply forget altogether that they need to be lifted up in prayer too. I might try to pat myself on the back for giving to some charity but then I have to take away that very patting because I fail to give a friend the praise they so deserve on any given day. I try to be good, to never sin, to listen to the spirit's prodding. Yet, I often fail and then fail again.

What gets me is that I do this over and over. I know it is just me putting the cart before the horse. I'm a little fickle and a little whimsical and a little eccentric I guess because when I pray and I ask God to forgive me for my sins, I sometimes fail to even remember the way I forgot to give a friend their due praise. God reminds me though and when He reminds me I always feel like such a dope. Why couldn't I see how that friend needed my sincere appreciation, affection or kindness? Why couldn't I see how they needed ME?

Day 17

I might not always see the light, but it isn't because He isn't shining. He shines softly and tenderly on my every thought. I just have to see! But, sometimes He has to blind me!

Acts 13:11 (KJV) And now, behold, the hand of the Lord is upon thee, and thou shalt be blind, not seeing the sun for a season. And immediately there fell on him a mist and a darkness; and he went about seeking some to lead him by the hand.

PRAYER

Dear Father of grace, I whisper my praise throughout every moment, throughout every season, throughout those times when Your light truly is blinding—and I deserve to be blinded just like Paul—because I have failed to show the love that You poured over my heart and soul, the love that You taught me to give without thought for my own needs or desires. You remind me, so many times, that this love You poured out on my life—this love that came about because of Your sacrifice—is a love that is meant to be shared with those I meet along my path. I'm tempted to forget that this love is the very thing that I need to bring to those I know who are in need, those who are hurting or doubting, those who are burdened with struggles I know nothing about. This love You gave me is a love that doesn't stop at my heart's door. Like liquid, poured out on the spirit, it should splash over those I meet, drenching them, quenching their thirst for a taste of Your gentleness. Help me, Father, to reach out to those in need with the very same blessing, the very same love, that You soaked my soul in when I came to You, humble and broken, begging for the chance to enter into Your peace. Thank You, God, for saving me!

Day 18

I GIVE THINGS AWAY. Sometimes the things are little treasures I've had for years and other times there just a bauble that collects dust and tears. Either way, I give things to those who happen upon them and mention their fondness for the prize. Sometimes I have given away things that were more important to me than others but still, I've not regretted the giving—even when, later on, I needed whatever it was I gave to someone. Most often, I'm happy that I could give someone I love or someone in need a little bit of love through the gift that I hope to be a blessing to their heart and spirit.

It happened, though, that a little girl I know and love became interested in products from Bath and Body Works. As a fan of the products from this store, I had several of their lotions hidden away in my bathroom waiting for the time when I'd decide to use them. Well, when this little one mentioned her delight with the lotions, I thought that I would give her a couple of mine. My time with her was soon over and I failed, to my shame, to offer her the gifts of some of my Bath and Body Works products. All that evening and the next morning, I fretted because of my failure. There wasn't a doubt in my mind that the Lord had intended me to bless this child, but I had failed, not only myself—not only the little girl, but God himself. I had failed to give the way my soul had meant for me to and I was regretting my lack of generosity.

Finally, during my morning devotions time, I wrote her mother an email and told her to please remind me the next time we got together to share some of the lotions with her little girl, who I love so very much—like she was a child of my own blood. But, I won't stop there. If, by chance, the email is forgotten or unseen for some reason, I'll text and tell her the same thing. I am certain that God intended me to bless this little girl and I won't fail her or Him again.

It may seem like a little thing, this need to give from my heart—whatever it might be, lotions or love—the gifts are meant to be given with an open heart and an open hand and I refuse to let the miserable, miserly, mean spirited demon of stinginess get his claws into the gift I've always been blessed with—the gift of giving is something that I know God intended for me and even though what I give is not really important or spectacular, these gifts are meant to bless and reflect the overpowering grace, the blessings, that I've been given throughout my life. The gifts I give aren't so much a sacrifice as a surrender of my sinful nature—in the natural man, I am stingy and wouldn't give anything at all. But, because I follow Jesus, I remember that it is better to give than receive and that giving is something that blesses me even more than it blesses the one I give to.

I won't forget the next time God urges me to give—because without that blessing of giving, I'd never know the meaning of a generous spirit.

Matthew 7:11 (KJV) If ye then, being evil, know how to give good gifts unto your children, how much more shall your Father which is in heaven give good things to them that ask him?

PRAYER

Dear Lord, please help me to always remember the joy that comes to me and the one I give to—when I follow Your urging and respond with giving. Please never let me forget the ways You have blessed me so completely and the ways, even though they're small ways, that I can bless others. Help me to always follow Your example and give with all my heart and soul, the wonder of a love that I always hope will control me. Thank You for giving me the gift of a Savior that has brought more light and love to my life than I can possibly thank You for. He is the reason I smile, the reason I

Day 18

try, the reason I know that, with Him, all things certainly are possible and all the world is a open door—when I remember who is in control of it. I love You, Lord and want to thank You for providing me the wisdom to know that when I give to anyone—I give to You, my light and my love, the miracle who is my eternal home.

Day 19

I came from a Christian background. My Mama never doubted that Jesus was the way, the truth, the life. My granny never gave her worship to any other. Jesus was her One and only. My great grandmother was just as pious and she happened to be an old timey preacher's daughter.

That preacher who was named Jeff King, traveled over the Blue Ridge Mountains on horseback, moving from place to place, from community to community, preaching the gospel. He was so dedicated I've heard stories of how, during the Winter months when he visited churches across the region, his boots had to be pried loose from his stirrups because they were frozen in place. He was assuredly a preacher who could preach and I would love to hear him. Just as assuredly, there is the promise of heaven when I will have that opportunity. I don't know if there is a need for preaching in heaven but I'm pretty sure I'll learn just how much he loved our Lord when I get there.

Since I came from a Christian background you might think I had some special key to grace that others don't have. You would be completely wrong about that. I had to come to Jesus at the cross, bend my knee and repent of my sins. I had to be forgiven the same way each one who expects to enter heaven's gates one day must be. It's not hard to gain forgiveness though. Just ask God and just believe in your heart that He is the One who can save you and He will save you. He will put all your sins under the blood, washing away all the filth of that sin and replacing that filth with a gift that was love breathed. The gift of salvation is a gift that can't be bought or sold. It can't be earned and it can't be lost.

Day 19

Once you're saved, you're truly saved. You don't have to worry about that problem of sin anymore. Jesus bought us and He won't let us go!

John 10:28 (KJV) And I give unto them eternal life; and they shall never perish, neither shall any man pluck them out of my hand.

PRAYER

Dear Lord, Thank You for saving me. Please help me to always remember Your words that tell me You will never let me go. With You, I have found the answer to every prayer, the comfort when I am down, the joy when I weep, the light in the darkness. With You, dear Lord, I have found more than hope. I have found more than joy. I have found peace and love that defies all wisdom. It is peace and love that reveals sin to me and helps me to overcome that same sin. It is the assurance that You have loved me with a undying love and that You have forgiven me so that I am forever Yours! I love You, Lord and could never thank You enough for the wonder of salvation that is forever mine, salvation that is the gift I will forever delight in. Thank You, Lord—for YOU!

Day 20

I TEXT OR CALL my mom every morning around 7. I think what got that started was when I went through a divorce from my first husband and she was worried about me. Back then, because it was the time she went to work, I texted her around 5 am. That is early but that was when she was getting ready and it was the best time to text or call because after that she would be on the job. I worked as a newspaper delivery driver and I was out and about anyway so that time worked well for me too.

I know why she worried about me then. I worried about me then! I was a mess. I didn't eat right. I was still addicted to cigarettes. I even had moments of doubt when I drank alcohol. I was, literally, a mess. I couldn't focus and the job at the newspaper was about the only job I could do with all the anxiety and fear that was darkening my life. I was not in church and that, too, was enough to depress me. One plus in my life then was that every night as I drove my paper route (about 4 hours of the night) I listened to The Light FM, (Billy Graham's radio station), and heard God's music and God's teaching. That and my mom's constant love was the encouragement that poured out just enough sanity into my spirit to keep me from moving out of the light into total darkness.

During that period I can still remember several times when I fell to my knees as tears poured out of me like rivers of sorrow. I was so devastated that the grief rained down through my spirit and seemed to bore holes into my soul. I begged God to help me. I begged Him for some kind of relief. I begged Him to make this pain go away and allow me to find a way to be my old self. When I think of it, though, that old self wasn't someone I really wanted to

Day 20

be. It was then that I believe God began to work on me for real. He changed me from the inside out! If you let Him change you, you won't ever be disappointed with the results—He is assuredly the best of the best when it comes to CREATING!

Psalm 51:10 (KJV) Create in me a clean heart, O God; and renew a right spirit within me.

PRAYER

Dear Lord, I know You are the One who made me to begin with so I know You have the answers for every situation I get myself into. I'm asking You, with these words—to please help, please answer, please bless everyone who reads this and finds themselves in similar situations, going through dark days and climbing steep terrain… help them like You helped me and CREATE the beauty that only YOU know how to create. With Your ingenuity, Your light, Your love, create something beautiful from the parts of our lives that make us feel so lost and alone. Give us hope when we're walking through the sorrow and show us the way toward a brighter tomorrow. YOU are the only one who can bring beauty from the pain and YOU have the answers to the bleakest rain. I will follow You, Lord—WE will follow YOU—through everything. Thank You, Lord, for being the answer—for grace to sustain as You bless even the grief with gain.

Day 21

SOMETIMES LIFE GETS IN the way of my relationship with the One who makes my life worthwhile. I get caught up in shopping, writing, reading, socializing or any number of other things and don't keep my mind stayed on Christ, the creator of all those good things. It is then that the pleasures of sin pulls me in.

Addiction is a sin yet a sin that I've partaken of more times than I care to count. Just when I think I've overcome this devilish darkness I find myself overcome by the sin again. It comes in so many forms. It comes as food, alcohol, nicotine—and, yes, even shopping. There are even addictions to exercise and the good things of the world. We never know just where an addiction may lurk until we realize we're a full blown addict and we have to start praying for a way through the darkness.

I have rid myself of many of the worst addictions. I'm not addicted to drugs or alcohol. I kicked cigarettes and there went the nicotine addiction. I'm not addicted to sex or food (although I could loose a few pounds and not be skinny). But I am still working on my addiction to shopping. It may sound silly but those shopping sprees that seem so harmless can lead to financial ruin and that is where shopping has steadily taken me. I still have everything I need but I have to use every spare dime for bills because I used all my time to shop for such a long time.

And these addictions get in the way of the Savior! His light shines brightly into the darkest parts of my heart and He is always illuminating the shadows and showing me the ways I need to change so that His light can shine brighter in this world I live in. I love my Jesus and am so thankful that He shows me how I fail Him each and every day. Without Him showing me the ways I need to change and pray I would never find my way to the joy of that loving bond with the One who created me to give my love away!

1 Samuel 25:28 (KJV) I pray thee, forgive the trespass of thine handmaid: for the Lord will certainly make my lord a sure house; because my lord fighteth the battles of the Lord, and evil hath not been found in thee all thy days.

PRAYER

Dear Father in heaven, remember me and lead me—where my heart can feel the joy of Your loving kindness, where my soul knows what it means to breathe the rich silence of innocence and purity, where the gentle of faith makes a way for me to feel the lingering grace that You whisper through my soul. Please never let me go—because in my heart, I know that You are the One who can make a way where no way has been found. You can destroy the demons that assault my mind and heart with a beautiful that only comes to those who know You are the beauty found in every feeling, every expression, every gesture. You are the reason, the answer, the love that uplifts and soothes, reassuring me that—even though this world is evil—there is still good to be found when I look around at the people who know YOU, the only way to know real hope. Thank YOU, Lord, for love that never grows old.

Day 22

THERE ARE TIMES WHEN I just wish I could disappear. Like when I don't have enough money to pay my bills. I know Peter and I know Paul and I've done my fair share of robbing the one to pay the other one. It isn't a fun place to be in life but it is a place I've been several times. And when I'm there, how I wish I could just hide!

When the bills weigh more than the money that is there to pay them there is a problem. What should you do when you just don't have enough to go around? Should you borrow? Should you beg? Should you wish or hope or pray? That praying. That is what I do and that is when I find the most help for my finances. Praying works wonders and praying brings hope to the hopeless. Praying is my answer to my financial woes and praying is the place that allows me to remember just how blessed I am—despite these financial griefs.

As I've struggled along in my life, I've learned to let go of things that don't really matter. These things include many material possessions because they absolutely do not matter. Yes, like most of us, I like buying pretty things and owning pretty things. It's fun to dress nice and decorate and eat out and go to a movie, etc. etc. etc. But there are times when it is better to give up material things and, instead, have your finances make sense.

When I need to give some things up, I do it with the assurance that what I'm doing is for a higher purpose, the greater good, for God's kingdom, where I'm the best I can be and where I know that God will sanctify me with grace that shows me I am His child. He is my guide and I know that, through His leading, I will grow spiritually, personally and financially. Even if I need to give some

Day 22

"things" up, I am gaining something much better in the long run. God is so good and I praise Him!

1 Timothy 6:10 (KJV) For the love of money is the root of all evil: which while some coveted after, they have erred from the faith, and pierced themselves through with many sorrows.

PRAYER

Dear Lord, Know my heart and soul. Silence the worries, the fears and tears with Your amazing love, Your grace and peace, the joy that comes from knowing, with You, anything and everything is possible. When I let my troubles drain my hope and struggles become great so I can't cope, I remember that YOU are with me. Through the worst that comes, through everything that tears at my faith, through the cruelty of darkness that I don't know how to face. . . You are with me, giving me the ability to face whatever comes with confidence that, as long as I listen to You and abide in faith, Your amazing grace will fill my life with more reasons to praise than I can possibly imagine. As long as I have You, Lord, nothing else really matters. You are the reason, the answer, the wonder that erases every anxiety. You are my light in the darkness, the One who never abandons me, the One who is there when the whole world is stormy and unsettled. You are the ONE I know I can count on and for that, I am so very thankful!

Day 23

WHEN I FIRST STARTED to put my heart on the empty page, I was at a loss for words when it came to those times when I didn't really have the thoughts, the dreams, the means, the message to fill up the pages. I was lost amid the words and the thoughts weren't flowing like they should have. I wasn't able to think up what to place on that empty page and when the time came to stop writing I realized that I hadn't put anything meaningful down on that blank page.

I needed inspiration and it would take years for me to realize that my inspiration wasn't found in my heart where there was plenty to write about. For me, inspiration came to life when I began seeking God the hardest, with a heart that yearned for Him the way plants yearn for water. I needed Him more than I needed my own soul. He was the answer to my prayers, the life beneath my dreams, the hope that made me aware I could overcome anything.

When I searched for Him with my whole heart and gave Him all my attention, He poured out His blessings on my heart and filled me up with a joy that I had never known before. He flooded my life with kindness, inspiration, enlightenment, faith, fulfillment, every good thing I could imagine He blessed me with. To say the least, I was in awe of Him. He was, He is—indeed, pure love.

His love shone on my face. He washed me in feelings of sincerity and faith, freeing me from the shadows of pain and sorrow, destroying all the worries that had forever haunted me. He awoke in me an inspiration to write that I had never known before and poetry and prose drenched my empty pages like they had never done before. The more I wrote, the more I wrote, the more I wrote and I know God lit a fire under me—when I searched for Him with my whole heart—so I literally glowed from the presence that was HIM.

Exodus 34:29 (KJV) And it came to pass, when Moses came down from mount Sinai with the two tables of testimony in Moses' hand, when he came down from the mount, that Moses wist not that the skin of his face shone while he talked with him.

PRAYER

Dear Lord, If You hadn't placed Your love, Your joy, Your peace inside of me, I wouldn't know the meaning of shining my light to a cold and dark world. Because You placed YOU inside me, I know what it means to show others the love of Christ, the joy that never subsides, the peace that is a part of my life. Because of YOU, I know the meaning of faith, hope and love and because of You, I can shine like the morning sun. With a glow that comes from being with You, Lord, I know that what others see when they see me is the presence of the Master, the Creator, the inspiration for everything I am and all that I can ever be. Because of You living inside me, I can face anything that comes my way with a light that never fades because Your love is an everlasting love, a forever promise, a eternal grace. . . because of YOU, I can face tomorrow with the assurance that, most assuredly, everything will work out as You planned it and I need not ever worry about what might happen. Thank You, Lord. . . I love YOU more than I can possibly say in words.

Day 24

I LIKE TO WORK in wood for the woodstove. We sometimes buy a load of logs and my husband saws them into the right size and, together, (using a wood splitter) we split and stack the wood in our shed where it waits until the winter months to be used. There is no better heat than the wood heat that leaves your warm all the way to your bones. I love it!

Some people might think of this work as too hard or demanding and it is a challenge to physically exert yourself for the time it takes to cut, split and stack a load of wood. Not to mention the exertion used when bringing it in and loading the woodstove. Yes. This process does take some work but I've learned, over the years, that most things that are worthwhile do take a bit of work. If it's too easy it's usually not worth my time.

Just like cutting and splitting a load of firewood, breathing life into a heart who has been hurt by pain and sorrow can take some time and even hard work. Being the encourager usually means taking time to give back to a heart who is in need. It means finding just the right words, the right places, the right ideas and the right kindness. It means giving back to someone with a heart that is in tune with the Holy Spirit because it is Him who leads us in any true heart work we do. It is Him who brings us the wisdom to share a part of His grace with someone who is lingering in heartbreak.

With a bit of work, though, we can encourage a heart who is in pain. Through prayer and a heart who listens to His wisdom, we have it in us to give hope to the hopeless, faith to the faithless and love to the one who is lost in hatred. We have it in us, through Him, to make a way where there seemed to be no way, to color a

Day 24

pain in hues of grace and to blend feelings of joy and inspiration so they erase every shadow.

Psalms 126:5 (KJV)—They that sow in tears shall reap in joy.

PRAYER

Dear Lord, King of my thoughts, my heart, my soul—please remind me when I'm not sure which word to speak, which thought to hear, which gift to bring—that Your light is the only light I need to reveal the encouragement, the help, the lifting up of a heart. Your light will shine so brightly that I can see through the darkness into the inspiration that You bring, the kindness that You stir, the beauty that comes from knowing the wonder of Your unconditional love. Because You are with me wherever I go, there is no doubt that I have what it takes to bring a smile to a face, a joy to a heart, gladness to a soul. Because of You, dear Lord, I can face the world with the hope of giving something only Your love could rouse. Because of YOU, I can give a love that is better than any gift there is. And, because of You, dear Jesus. . . I know that the gift I give others is a gift created by a love that will last forever! Thank You, Lord—You're the gift my soul will always treasure.

Day 25

HAVE YOU EVER DOUBTED your salvation? No? Well I have. I've doubted to the point of asking Him to come into my heart again and repenting of those sins that have long ago been forgiven. I'm not sure where that anxiety over my salvation comes from but I'm pretty certain it comes from the need to KNOW FOR SURE that I'm saved. It's such an amazing and important and needed thing. Salvation! It is the only way to end up in an eternity—in heaven, the place I hope to go. It is the only way to avoid hell and punishment that lasts forever, eternally. It is the only way to make it home to Jesus and that love that my heart yearns for. Yes, oh yes. Salvation is so very important.

I've listened to so many sermons on salvation and I'm always a little more tuned into the ones that tell me, yes, people do doubt their salvation and need to be reminded that once God saves you, you're saved. You can't do it again. You don't need to do it again. It is forever and always. It is eternal. And all the worrying in the world won't change it. Not that there aren't people who should be worrying. If someone is claiming to be saved and they're still deeply planted in a sinful life, I might worry. Yes. We all sin. But when God saves you, He pulls you out of that sin mire too—eventually—and He gives you a new heart, a new life. You are a new creation.

What I've learned, from my own studies and from those preachers I've heard preaching on salvation and the way people doubt their salvation, I've come to understand that it isn't always a bad thing to question. If you question, it might be sure that you truly have been saved to the uttermost. That questioning is your heartfelt need to be certain that you have access to Jesus and eternal life. It means more to you than assuming a confidence that might not be the most important thing after all. The most important thing, in all truth, is your soul's destiny!

Philippians 2:12 (KJV) Wherefore, my beloved, as ye have always obeyed, not as in my presence only, but now much more in my absence, work out your own salvation with fear and trembling.

PRAYER

Dear Lord, thank You for coming to this earth, for living and dying on a old rugged cross, so that I could be saved to the uttermost. Thank You, LORD, for saving me. I can't say it too many times. Thank You, Lord, for saving me. It is the most valuable gift I've ever been given and it is the most precious thing that I've ever experienced. Through Your kindness, Your grace, Your love, You gave me a new life, a new hope, a new heart. You taught me what it means to listen to the voice of One who abides in my heart, silences my doubts and reassures me that, YES, OH YES—You have saved me and I never have to fear death. Thank You, Lord, for giving me the most beautiful gift of all, salvation from, not only hell (although salvation from hell is more important than I could even imagine)—but life without the One who makes a way where no way could be found. Thank You, Lord, for saving me and giving me a reason to live this life, FOR YOU, my Savior, my King, my forever! Thank You, Lord, for loving me!

Day 26

WHEN I WORK ON some project, whatever it might be, I don't stop until it's done. I might pull away from the project to rest but I always come back in due time. I don't give up. I get the job done. I'm not satisfied until it is finished.

Jesus spoke the words "It is finished" from the cross, just before He gave up the ghost. He said Tetelestai—"It is finished" or "Paid in Full." Finally, our sin debt was cleared and Jesus could rest. His job was completed. He had done His duty and we could be saved from eternity without God. And I'll never be able to thank Him enough for saving me.

When I finish a project I feel satisfied, content, fulfilled. I imagine Jesus must have felt that way too. He had done a job no one else who lived or had ever lived or who would ever live could do. His job was one that only God himself could have completed. And He had done this job without complaint or protest. He had taken the punishment that had been ours to feel. Only we didn't have to feel it. He had saved us from the debt we owed. God only knows what we owe Him for what He's done for our souls!

I often find myself thinking that if I do this or that—will it make Jesus happy. If I complete some project, will the Lord smile down at me? If I do a good job, will His light shine across my spirit? If I do this or that to His liking, will He bless me in a way that I can feel? I yearn to please Him and I find myself seeking ways that I believe the Holy Spirit is leading me to do just that. And I don't have a doubt that He pours out blessings across my life that I might never realize or know to be thankful for. Blessings of hope, faith and love—peace, joy and wonder so amazing that I will always have a reason to be thankful! He is amazing! He is my Savior!

John 19:30 (KJV) When Jesus therefore had received the vinegar, he said, It is finished: and he bowed his head, and gave up the ghost.

PRAYER

Dear Heavenly Father, It is with a heart who is grateful beyond words that I offer You my thanks for giving me the grace to know the One who lived and died and sits on Your right hand, where He makes intercession for me when I don't even know what to pray. When the words won't come, thanks to Your Son, I don't have to speak. I only have to believe and I believe with all my heart that the love You pour out over those who believe in Jesus is a love that can't be found anywhere else. This is love that is beyond our understanding. It is a love that completes us and a love that sees us for who we truly are—and still gives us the hope to know love that is more beautiful than our thoughts or hearts can possibly describe. Because of You, my Father, my heart knows what it is to be blessed in ways that I can't even comprehend. Thank You, Father, for loving me beyond what my spirit can fathom, for loving me with a love that is beyond amazing. This love is the miracle of grace that only You could have demonstrated.

Day 27

REFLECTING ON MY LIFE, there have been so many times that I can't count them when I was sure I'd be drowned by the sorrows or burned up by the flames of pain. I know that I shouldn't let myself get into such a rut, but I have done this on numerous occasions. I've been depressed so badly that the entire world actually looked gray and dim—even through the light of an amazing sun. I couldn't see the joy for the fear and I couldn't taste the wonder for the tears. Being in a place like that is marked by shadows and dread, worry and disillusionment, panic that seems to color the entire world in so many phobias that nothing seems good or kind or hopeful anymore. I don't like being in that place. And it is not my plan to ever go back there again.

Because I've known the darkness, though, it's a smidgeon more beautiful in the light. I see the colors cresting my thoughts, the gentleness, the laughter, the joy, all the hues so brilliant and vibrant, working their way through my heart, soul and mind. This is something I had failed to notice before the darkness overtook me for a time. When I came out of the dark, though, I entered a light like no other. A light that is alive with grace and peace, inspirations so warm and welcoming they send tingles of thrilling emotions across my spirit. Without a doubt, I am blessed and, though I couldn't always see through the darkness, I know that I have always been blessed.

God is so amazing. He is like the whisper in the song, the silence when I'm alone, the goodness that can never go wrong. He sends me through the storms only to show me that He is there, living in my prayer, awaiting the moment when He can lift my heavy burden and replace it with a serenity that is like the breathe of love He caresses my soul with. He is—oh yes—He is an awesome God! I'm so thankful that He is mine and I am His.

Isaiah 26:17 (KJV) Like as a woman with child, that draweth near the time of her delivery, is in pain, and crieth out in her pangs; so have we been in thy sight, O LORD.

PRAYER

Dear Lord, You know me better than anyone else. You know me even better than I know myself. You see what I feel when I feel like my heart has been broken. You understand my brokenness and comfort me with Your kindness. You light up my spirit with Your consolation, relieve my burdens, send beauty through my dread. You make me feel like there is a answer—even when I'm unsure what to ask You. Because of Your love, Your grace, Your light—I'm filled with a faith that is alive like the timelessness flowing through Your breath, the same breath that breathed air into my lungs upon my birth, the same breath that silences the darkness with inspiration and brilliance. You are the whisper of hope that sings through my soul and I know that, because of You—my wonderful Savior, I can come back from the hurt, the worry, the doubt, into a place of glory, gratification, grace. Because I know You, dear Lord, I know hope even in the bleakest place. Thank You, Lord—for giving me the answers even when I wasn't sure how to ask.

Day 28

I'VE BEEN READING JOB. Job had a really hard time for a while. He was desperate, despairing, disappointed and flooded by darkness. His heart was still faithful though. In spite of all that pain and sorrow and even with his wife telling him to curse God and die, he was loyal to God. He was assuredly in a difficult place and I don't know how he felt because I've never had it that hard in my lifetime. Thankfully.

Even though I don't know what it's like to walk in Job's shoes, like most of us, I have had hard times. I've seen my dreams fall apart and my heart breaking. I've been deceived and felt darkness pour out like a thick syrup on my whole life. I've yearned for the chance to just walk, once more, on the mountain. And, still, the valley was my home for a time.

Nothing lasts forever, though (except GOD), so eventually I would find my way out of the dark place and feel the light of His glory falling across my thoughts, my mind, my heart and soul, everything that I'd known. And I was never more thankful to God than when I felt the joyful relief that is so overpowering and touches the heart like nothing else than when that sorrow and pain was released and I was reassured that He had blessed me with a new dawn, a new hope, a new joy. His blessing felt like rain falling after a long, thirsty drought. Indeed, it was a famine of the soul.

With this renewal of my heart and soul, I was sure to feel that blessed rain nurturing me and I was sure to grow. The growth wouldn't be overnight. But it would be. It would remind me that I had the strength, the courage, the faith that I needed to face life. Even when I had been through the storm, like Job, I knew that

Day 28

grace penetrated my darkness and left me with a glow that would remind others who were going through pain that the light would come again. They could hold onto their hope.

Job 42:10 (KJV) And the LORD turned the captivity of Job, when he prayed for his friends: also the LORD gave Job twice as much as he had before.

PRAYER

Dear Lord, There were so many times when I felt like the darkness had overwhelmed me to the point of complete despair. My heart was breaking, my mind was aching and my thoughts were making me feel like I couldn't possibly see through the dark into the light of a new dawn. Those were the moments when my heart cried out for God's relief, for His comfort, for my faith to sustain me through the storms that silenced every prayer with doubt and left me feeling like I had no way out of the pain. But, despite my struggles and my failures, all the reasons I had for depression—He came through for me. In time, He wrote His love across my thoughts and reassured me so that I knew there was renewal. There was hope. There was a second chance and, because of His love, His grace—I certainly was given twice as much as I had had in the past. Because of Him, I know what it is to be blessed and I confess, I've never been more amazed by the blessings He pours out over my spirit. He is a God who gives generously, gifts that I know hold more meaning than any gift I could have thought of myself. His gifts are made of hope, faith and love. His gifts restore the soul. His gifts are the answers to prayers and so wonderful that they answer prayers I never even spoke aloud, prayers that came from my soul, where His love overshadows every doubt or dark thought.

Day 29

AFTER I STARTED TAKING medication for my bipolar disorder, I realized that I wasn't nearly as creative. My heart and soul didn't go into my writings the way they once had. Where I once was so prolific and engaging, I was dull and boring. I couldn't make the words come out and only tried to write occasionally and with much difficulty. I told my counselor that I was fine except for the fact that my heart didn't pour out its emotions and thoughts on the empty page anymore. I was dead center in the middle of a bought of writer's block like I'd never experienced before.

Even though the words wouldn't come to me any longer, I was thankful for the medicine that had left me with the assurance that I wasn't just crazy the way I'd thought I was. I really did have an illness that I could pronounce and one that other people had so I could compare my emotions, doubts, dreams and worries with them. Other people felt like I did. So even though I could barely drum out a sentence on my computer, I was thankful to the One who I was sure had given me the cure for my dark and dreary struggles with depression and mania. Yes, I was definitely thankful.

It would be years before I felt like I could write again. There would be plenty of fear that I wouldn't be able to fill the pages with my poetry and prose and that God had taken that gift. I would go through moments of sorrow when it came to putting words down, but when He finally lifted the veil from my heart and the words started to pour forth, it felt like the morning sun kissing my soul. I was alive with the wonder, the freedom, the light that seemed to penetrate the shadows I'd been walking through. Finally, I could write again. Sometimes I wonder if that break from words was

Day 29

God's way of forcing me to appreciate what I had—the gift that He gave, His blessings on my life.

Psalms 51:10 (KJV) Create in me a clean heart, O God; and renew a right spirit within me.

PRAYER

Dear Lord, Thank YOU so much for the gifts You've poured out over my heart and soul, over my thoughts and hopes, over my dreams. Thank You for blessing me with creativity and insight, words that come from You, poetry and prose that were hidden away in my heart for a time, but now—are thriving and coming to life in my writings. You made me a woman who loves, not only words, but the memories, the dreams, the living that brought to life those writings that I know YOU inspired with Your kindness, Your grace, Your gifts to my soul. Because of You, Lord, I know the meaning of praise and because of You, I praise with a heart and soul that is devoted to You, the One who reminds me with every dawn that nothing on earth—no amount of creativity or insight—can compare to the miracle of Your vision for those who know the joy of a relationship with You, the One who created us all. Thank You, Lord, for Your love!

Day 30

THERE WAS A TIME when I wasn't nearly as close to the Lord as I am now. I didn't yearn for His instruction, His grace, His presence in the same way I do now. Yes, I always sought Him from my soul and I can see that I searched for Him in many places where I know now I would never find Him. But today I yearn for Him in every moment of every day. I seek Him out with my thoughts and my prayers, my faith and the awareness that GOD IS GOOD all the time. He is always, always, always good. When I seek Him, I am seeking that GOOD that is Him.

When I write a devotional or write a praise poem, I am sure that God is listening like a Father listens to a child. With bended ear, He hears the softest whisper of need in my soul and blesses me with enough grace to fill that need and, most often, more needs that I haven't even thought of. He is a good, good God. He is so GOOD! I am always in awe of His goodness, His GODNESS! He is such a wonderful Creator. He is such a incredible God. I am amazed by Him always.

Not only does He listen to me when I write. He listens to me when I pray and He listens to me when I hope and He listens to my faith and praise. He listens even when I don't speak or write or pray or think. He listens, even when I sleep. He never leaves me alone. He is always there, always aware, always full of care. He is wise and warm and willing to lead me through the storms and darkest fears that might haunt me or taunt me or make me feel like I can't when, with Him, I can.

There was a time when I didn't seek Him the way I should have. I didn't realize how much He meant to me. I wasn't aware of just how GREAT God is. Today, I know Him and I want Him with me, His light so brilliant it floods my spirit with love during every minute of the day. I'm grateful for this God I love with everything I have inside me. He is life to me.

Psalms 147:1 (KJV) Praise ye the LORD: for it is good to sing praises unto our God; for it is pleasant; and praise is comely.

PRAYER

Dear Lord, There isn't a doubt in my mind that You are worthy of praise. The wonder of YOU is so good that I could never think of enough words, enough thoughts, enough praise to do Your grace justice. You are the reason that I hope, the reason that I love, the reason that my praises are poured out for You. You are good in a way that words can't describe. Your goodness inspires, reassures, delights. Your goodness brings smiles, laughter, joy. Your goodness is so amazing that nothing I could ever think or say would be worthy of You. YOU, my precious Savior, are the miracle who gives compassion a definition. You are the One who smiles light through my soul. You are the reason that my heart knows what it is to love. Because of You, I truly adore. Thank You, Lord—for the blessing of Your love.

I'm Always Smiling...

I'm thankful for the moment
The reassurance that I'm blessed
With beautiful friends and family
Those who encourage me to do my best
I'm thankful for the canines
Who have trampled through my life
Leaving me with footprints of joy
To remind me that I'm alive
I'm thankful for the beauty
Of sunset, ocean, tree and plant
All the wonders of nature around us
Showing that life is assuredly miraculous
I'm thankful for the many gifts
Sent from heaven above to each of us
Gifts of hope, peace, faith and real love
To make us aware of the One who created us
I'm thankful for a deep relationship
With the One who died for my sins
He rose again to remind me that I can
Someday enter heaven to be with Him
I'm thankful for God's gift to me
The life that I've lived, His blessings
Through Jesus' love and friendship
Reminding me that He's always beside me
He is with me eternally and I am blessed
With more love than I could ever expect
Thanking God for HIS LOVE, HIS PEACE

I'm Always Smiling...

GRACE that flows through my heart—I believe
He is the answer to my every need
He is the blessing that will forever be
Walking across my thoughts, making
Footprints with His gentle love and light
He is alive and in my spirit, He abides
Writing His promises over my heart, my life!
He's the blessing that shines through my smile
Reflecting a love that is like a burning fire!